Table of Contents

Growing and Changing

When you were born you were small and helpless. Your family had to dress you. They had to feed and change you. But as you grow, you get stronger. Some kids may be taller or bigger than you. They may be able to do things you cannot, but that is okay. We are all special in many ways. How are you special?

Babies need adults to do almost everything.

▲ See how you grow!

▲ As you grow, you learn new things.

Many changes happen as you grow. To **grow** means to become bigger. You may get taller. You may gain weight. You may lose a tooth. A new one may grow in. As your body grows, your mind grows too. You learn new ideas in school. Maybe you learn to play a sport or the piano. How have you grown and changed?

Keep Growing

Do you know a teen? When you turn 13 you will be a teen too! Teens are older than children. Their bodies change. They look more like adults. Their minds and feelings change too. They learn to do the things adults do. They may have jobs or drive cars.

Teens spend time with their friends.

Your body will stop growing when you are an adult. But you never stop learning and changing. Adults change as they **age** or get older. Some adults may have more trouble hearing or seeing, as they get older. They may need special tools to help them get around. Most older people are healthy. They may enjoy doing some of the same things you do! What are some things you want to do when you are an adult?

You can learn from an older person.

Healthful Habits

Do you eat breakfast every day? Do you brush your teeth every day? A **habit** is something you do over and over again. Some habits help you stay healthy as you grow up.

Do you exercise most days after school? If you do, exercise is a habit. Exercise helps your bones and muscles grow. It makes you strong. It helps you feel good about yourself, too.

Reading is a healthful habit for your mind.

Here are some healthful habits.

- Eat breakfast every day.
- Choose healthful foods.
- Be active.
- Do not smoke or breathe in smoke.
- Get checkups from your doctor.
- Keep your body clean.
- Spend time with family and friends.
- Relax.
- Get plenty of rest and sleep.
- Read and think to use your mind.

Your Stomach

Eating healthful foods is a habit that helps you take care of your stomach. Your **stomach** is the body part that helps change food so your body can use it. Do you know why your stomach does this? It is so your body can use the food to help you grow up strong and healthy.

Your body gets energy from food. **Energy** is the power to work and play. Your stomach helps turn food into energy. Be sure to chew your food well before you swallow. Drink plenty of water! How can you take care of your stomach?

These children have energy for their day.

Your Bones and Muscles

You have more than 200 bones in your body! **Bones** are strong, hard body parts that give you support. Bones come in different shapes and sizes. You need to take care of all your bones to grow up healthy.

Keeping your bones strong can help you grow up healthy. Be active! It helps your bones grow stronger. Eat lots of milk and dairy foods to make your bones stay strong. Wear safety equipment when you play.

A broken bone may need a cast.

Stetching keeps your muscles loose.

Muscles are body parts that help you move. Your muscles grow, as you get older. Your muscles get stronger when you exercise.

Always stretch your muscles before and after being active! Stretching helps your muscles move easily. It can keep you from getting hurt. How can you help your muscles grow and stay healthy?

Your Heart and Lungs

Your **heart** is the body part that pumps blood. It is a muscle in the middle of your chest. Your heart pumps blood through blood vessels. **Blood vessels** are tubes that carry blood inside your body.

Exercise to keep your heart healthy. Your heart is a muscle. Exercise to keep it strong!

Eating healthful foods helps you have a healthy heart.

Exercise makes your lungs healthy.

Your body needs air to stay alive. **Lungs** are the body parts that bring air into your body. You have two lungs, one on each side of your chest. Air goes into your lungs when you breathe in. It leaves your lungs when you breathe out.

Keep your lungs and heart healthy. Stay away from smoke. When you breathe in through your nose and out your mouth it helps keep the air you breathe clean.

What are ways you can keep your heart and lungs healthy?

Your Brain

The **brain** is the body part that tells your body what to do. It sends messages all around your body through nerves.

Nerves are long, string-like body parts that carry messages to help you see, hear, smell, taste, touch, and move. Your brain helps you think, learn and remember things.

Sleep gives your brain time to rest.

PROTECT YOUR BRAIN

Your brain is protected by a hard bone called your skull. You still need to take care of your brain. Here are some ways.

- Wear a helmet when you ride a bike, skate, or play baseball.
- Don't breathe in glue or cleaners.
- Wear a seat belt in a car or bus.
- Keep using your brain to learn.

How do you take care of your brain?

Life Skills
Activity

Set Health Goals

No Bones About It

Exercise helps keep your bones and muscles healthy. Choose an activity like dancing or soccer. Set a health goal to do this activity each day for one week.

1. Cut a sheet of paper in the shape of a leg bone.
2. Write the activity you have chosen and your goal on the paper.
3. Write and draw how well you did.